Focusing on Forensics

Bassim Hamadeh, CEO and Publisher
Mary Jane Peluso, Senior Specialist Acquisitions Editor
Tim Pike, Project Editor
Abbey Hastings, Associate Production Editor
Jess Estrella, Senior Graphic Designer
Sara Schennum, Licensing Associate
Don Kesner, Interior Designer
Natalie Piccotti, Senior Marketing Manager
Kassie Graves, Vice President of Editorial
Jamie Giganti, Director of Academic Publishing

Printed in the United States of America.

ISBN: 978-1-5165-2719-9 (pbk) / 978-1-5165-2720-5 (br)

Focusing on Forensics

A Lab Workbook

Timothy A. Pycraft

Purdue University Northwest

Brief Contents

Detailed Contents

About the Author

Timothy A. Pycraft, CLPE, MS, is a forensic scientist with the Indiana State Police Laboratory. He received a Bachelor of Science degree in Biology from Grace College (Winona Lake, IN), and received a Master of Science degree in Biology from St. Joseph College (West Hartford, CT). Mr. Pycraft is a certified latent print examiner at the Lowell Regional Laboratory, specializing in fingerprints, footwear, and tire impressions. He has testified as an expert witness in the state and federal courts. He is also a lecturer (LT) at Purdue University Northwest in Hammond, Indiana, where he has been teaching in the Forensic Investigative Science program in the Chemistry and Physics Department since 2010.

Acknowledgments

The author would like to thank the many individuals that have had an influence on what went into this workbook. The author specifically thanks those at the Indiana State Police Lowell Regional Lab; Sergeant Gerald Michalak; and forensic scientists Erica Gilbert, Scott Owens, Sharon Pollock, Shawn Stur, Kris Sturgeon, and others. The author also thanks Marcus Montooth and John Vanderkolk for their many insights through this process. The author thanks his family for their constant love, support, and help in this project.

Preface

"One learns from books and example only that certain things can be done. Actual learning requires that you **do** those things."

—Frank Herbert

CHAPTER ONE

Introduction into Forensic Science

Lab 1-1 Forensic Science or Forensic Entertainment

OBJECTIVE This lab puts the students' knowledge to the test, giving them a feel of what is real forensic science and what is mere entertainment.

DIRECTIONS Take the following quiz and test your knowledge in the area of forensic science.

Circle the correct answer.

The CSI Effect Quiz

T F Forensic scientists work the crime scene, process the evidence, interrogate suspects, and testify in court.

T F Every case gets solved thanks to the mountains of evidence at every crime scene.

T F Different partial fingerprint impressions can be "pieced together" using the AFIS system to find a suspect.

T F When evidence from a crime scene has its "chain of custody" broken, the evidence may be inadmissible in court.

T F An alternate light source will make all evidence fluoresce.

T F DNA results can be processed in an hour with the new technology available.

T F A forensic analyst can be trained in more than one area or discipline.

T F Color tests, gas chromatography, TLC, HPLC, and infrared spectrophotometry are all confirmatory tests used to identify drugs.

T F Footwear impressions will be an exact match when compared back to the shoe that created them.

T F Class characteristics are essential for identification, while individual characteristics may be similar to other individual characteristics.

T F Bloodstain pattern analysis is relatively simple to analyze, and interpretation can be done with as little as a few drops of blood.

T F A forensic scientist should be careful to only testify in the discipline in which he or she works.

Lab 1-2 Know Thy Paperwork!

OBJECTIVE Expose students to the abundance of paperwork that is involved with casework.

DIRECTIONS Using the correct forms, fill out the correct paperwork.

The following forms are used in different stages of processing the crime scene:

The ***Crime Scene Log*** is used at a crime scene once it has been secured. It is important to know who is going in and out of the crime scene. A crime scene should have (if possible) a single entrance and exit; that way there can be control of who has access to the crime scene.

The ***Property Record and Receipt*** form is used to record all items collected from a crime scene.

The ***Photography Log*** is used to document all the photos that were taken at a crime scene.

The ***Request for Laboratory Examination*** is used to inform what laboratory exams an agency wants on the evidence of a case.

Crime Scene Documentation

Forensic science is hyped with great amounts of interest and intrigue. However, with all the "fun" stuff comes a lot of paperwork. While it is not the most "glamorous" part of the job, it is the most important. You and others must depend on the accuracy of your notes, report, and evidence. The case—most importantly its outcome—hinges on it. If there are mistakes, errors, omissions, or doubt, it will ultimately impact the outcome within the courts.

Scenario

Investigation officer: You	Agency: PNW Forensics	PE - 9347
Case type: Burglary	Case number: 17PNW-00001	
Date of occurrence: Today	Time: Current	

There has been a burglary at the Z Grill located at Broadway Ave, Righthere, IN. The burglary was discovered by the manager, Ben Bear, at 0600 hours. When he arrived at work, he noticed the rear door had been pried open. There was a crow bar on the ground next to the door. He then called 911 and Officer Dooley arrived and took the original report. The weather is cool, 50°F with a light rain. Dispatch has assigned you to the burglary. You are requested to find Officer Dooley at the scene; he will inform you with more from there.

Upon your arrival, Officer Dooley advises you that the rear door had been pried open to gain entry. The money is kept in a safe in the manager's office. However, it appears the room was never accessed in the burglary. There are pry marks on and around the door, but it remains securely locked. Some damage was done in the dining area and some display memorabilia was found vandalized on the floor, along with another crowbar. Other than that, it seems nothing else is missing. Photography of the scene was taken using your Nikon D2Xs camera.

You are to write a report based on this information. "Process" the scene. You will "collect" evidence and "take photos" of what you deem important. (**The evidence you collect and the photos you take will be imaginary.**)

Use the following worksheets:

- Crime Scene log
- Property Record and Receipt
- Photography Log
- Laboratory Submission Request

CRIME SCENE LOG

Investigating agency ____________________

Support agencies ____________________

Case number ____________________

Location ____________________

Name	**Agency**	**IN Date/Time**	**OUT Date/Time**	**Reason for Entry**

PHOTOGRAPHY LOG			
Case number	**Agency**	**Date**	**Time**
Investigator		**Equipment**	
Crime type	**Location**		

Image number	**Description of photo**

<table>
<tr><th colspan="6">PROPERTY RECORD AND RECEIPT</th></tr>
<tr><td colspan="3">Name of investigating officer</td><td>PE</td><td colspan="2">Case/Incident number</td></tr>
<tr><td colspan="3">Name of submitting officer</td><td>PE</td><td colspan="2">Lab number</td></tr>
<tr><td colspan="2">Date</td><td>Time</td><td colspan="3">From</td></tr>
<tr><td colspan="5">Location</td><td>County</td></tr>
<tr><td colspan="6">Witness of recovery</td></tr>
<tr><td colspan="5">Details</td><td>Offense</td></tr>
</table>

RMS	Item #	Description (include quantity, color, serial numbers, and/ or identifying marks)

REQUEST FOR LABORATORY EXAMINATION

PNW Forensics **Lab Case #** ______________

Investigating officer	Email address	
Contributing agency		**County**
Address		**Telephone**
Type of investigation		**Agency case #**
Victim name(s)		
Suspect name(s)		
Case/Incident summary		
Court date	**Date of seizure**	**Assigned to**

Item #	Description of the Item Submitted	Examination request

Study Guide Summary Notes

The following summary notes are based on the lectures from Mr. Pycraft on the introduction of forensic science.

Define forensic science.

In the simplest terms, forensic science is the application of what two areas?
__________________ and _____________________

What areas of science make up forensic science? Are there a specific number of areas? Explain.

List some of the main disciplines that a crime lab may offer as a service.

__________________ __________________ __________________

__________________ __________________ __________________

__________________ __________________ __________________

Name a few "specialty" areas of forensics that are important but might not be available at the crime lab. In this case, an expert in that specialty would need to be hired.

__________________ __________________ __________________

__________________ __________________ __________________

What is important about the chain of custody?

What does a forensic scientist do?

____________ and ____________ physical evidence collected from the scene.

____________ questions about collection, packaging, identification, and reports interpretation of evidence.

Conducts ____________ for law enforcement agencies and other organizations.

Provides ____________ ____________ ____________ when called on for court.

Important terms:

Forensic science –

CSI effect –

Locard's principle of exchange –

Chain of custody –

Forensic scientist –

Certification –

Accreditation –

Additional Reading

Research a famous case or a local case in the newspaper/online. Look to see which discipline or disciplines were successful in helping solve the crime. Use the following questions as guidance:

- What type of crime occurred?
- What evidence was mentioned in the case?
- What forensic disciplines were involved (or likely involved)?
- Was the case solved? How was it solved?

Additional Resources

What does it take?

Ever wonder what it takes to become a forensic scientist? It does depend on what area you work in. Listed are classes that are recommended/required for some of the specific disciplines. All forensic jobs usually require a baccalaureate degree in a natural science or forensic science.

DNA: Genetics, Biochemistry, Molecular Cell Biology, and Statistics

Drug chemist: Chemistry, Organic Chemistry, Analytical Chemistry/instrumental methods

Fingerprints: Biology and Chemistry

Firearms: Chemistry and Physics

Trace: Analytical Chemistry/instrumental methods, Physics, Chemistry, Organic Chemistry

CHAPTER TWO

Crime Scene

Lab 2-1 What Kinds of Things Are Evidence?

OBJECTIVE Help students depict potential pieces of evidence from various crime scenes.

DIRECTIONS Examine the photos provided by your instructor. Determine the scenario the photos depict.

Photo ID: ______________________________

Type of crime: ______________________________

Crime against: PERSON or PROPERTY

How would you secure this scene?

____

____

____

What difficulties do the photos depict for this scene? How would you overcome them?

____

____

____

Which type of search pattern would you use in this scenario to ensure all potential evidence can be found? Why?

____

____

From the photos, what would be your main pieces of evidence that you would collect from this scene? What laboratory examinations would you want performed on them?

EVIDENCE	LAB EXAM

Photo ID: ______________________________

Type of crime: ______________________________

Crime against: PERSON or PROPERTY

How would you secure this scene?

____

____

____

What difficulties do the photos depict for this scene? How would you overcome them?

____

____

____

Which type of search pattern would you use in this scenario to ensure all potential evidence can be found? Why?

____

____

____

From the photos, what would be your main pieces of evidence that you would collect from this scene? What laboratory examinations would you want performed on them?

EVIDENCE	**LAB EXAM**

Photo ID: ______________________________

Type of crime: ______________________________

Crime against: PERSON or PROPERTY

How would you secure this scene?

____

____

____

What difficulties do the photos depict for this scene? How would you overcome them?

____

____

____

Which type of search pattern would you use in this scenario to ensure all potential evidence can be found? Why?

____

____

____

From the photos, what would be your main pieces of evidence that you would collect from this scene? What laboratory examinations would you want performed on them?

EVIDENCE	LAB EXAM

Lab 2-2 Photography

OBJECTIVE Teach students about what types of photos are needed to document evidence from a crime scene.

DIRECTIONS With the camera provided by your instructor, or with the one on your cell phone, complete the following:

360 photography

- Take overall photos of your classroom. Make sure to include all sides of the room so that someone could get a 360-degree feel from the photos
- Photograph all entry points into the classroom
- Take medium-range photos of your group area
- Take close-up photos of your group table
- Take close-up photos of your group table with a scale

Exterior photography

- Photograph your school building. Make sure to include all sides
- Photograph all entrances/exits to the building

Vehicle photography

- Photograph a vehicle. Make sure to include all sides
- Photograph make and model
- Photograph the VIN number

- Photograph license plate

Advanced Photography

- Photograph a fingerprint off a mirror surface
- Photograph evidence on curved surfaces
- Photograph a water mark

PHOTOGRAPHY LOG			
Case number	**Agency**	**Date**	**Time**
Investigator		**Equipment**	
Crime type	**Location**		

Image Number	Description of Photo

PHOTOGRAPHY LOG			
Case number	**Agency**	**Date**	**Time**
Investigator		**Equipment**	
Crime type	**Location**		

Image Number	**Description of Photo**

Lab 2-3 Search Patterns

OBJECTIVE Expose students to different methods that make searching for evidence efficient and systematic.

DIRECTIONS In this lab, choose the most appropriate/effective way to search the crime scene. Explain your answer.

Grid search	Line search
Zone search	Spiral search

1. A bedroom in a two-story family home with a victim in the master bathroom.

   ____

   Why? ______________________________

   ____

2. A body found in a retention pond.

   ____

   Why? ______________________________

   ____

3. "Shots fired," covering a two-block radius.

   ____

   Why? ______________________________

   ____

4. An unattached shed where tools were kept.

   ____

   Why? ______________________________

   ____

5. I-80/94 (westbound) between Cline exit and Kennedy exit.

   ____

   Why? ______________________________

   ____

6. A vehicle with the driver's-side window broken out.

   ____

   Why? ______________________________

   ____

Lab 2-4 Sketches

OBJECTIVE Let students understand how sketches aide in perspective of a scene.

DIRECTIONS In this lab, you will complete two sketches:

1. The classroom (primary crime scene)
   a. Entry points
   b. Length and width of room
   c. Evidence mentioned in scenario (next)
2. An overall of all additional linked crime scenes

Using the pictures found in figures 2.1–2.6 (photographs provided by your teacher), you will need to locate these areas of secondary crime scenes/additional locations and add them in your overall sketch.

Scenario:

Earlier this morning, a distillery was found set up in the rear ventilation hood in **class lab 232**. It was determined that it is likely "a class project" or maybe a disgruntled student who didn't get into Dr. P's **Brewing class**. Much of the glassware used in the setup was removed from **Lab 208**. Further investigation showed there was no forced entry into the door into Lab 208. In front of the hood, in room 232, there are visible muddy footwear impressions. Additional, similar muddy footwear impressions are visible in and around the **stairwell in 2SO2** as well as **classroom 223**. Left in the classroom was a backpack belonging to a student from Dr. S's Thermal Physics class. He stated that he had a meeting with Dr. S in the **Department of Chemistry and Physics office (251)** after class and must have forgotten it.

While interviewing students and staff, it was found that the secretary of the **Biological Science Department (298)** did see an individual walking through the hall with a cart of glassware, but thought nothing of it. She does not remember what the individual looked like. She only remembered because one of the pieces fell off and broke, which startled her.

Things to Consider

What is the estimated distance between Lab 208 and Room 232? From 223 to 232?

____

____

What other access points does the lab in 208 have?

____

____

Do you think this was done by a student? Why or why not?

____

What pieces of evidence do you give the most weight in this case so far (with the information at hand)?

____

____

Class Lab
232

Chemistry
Lab
208

2S02
STAIRS

Classroom
223

Department of
Chemistry &
Physics
251

Department of
Biological
Sciences
298

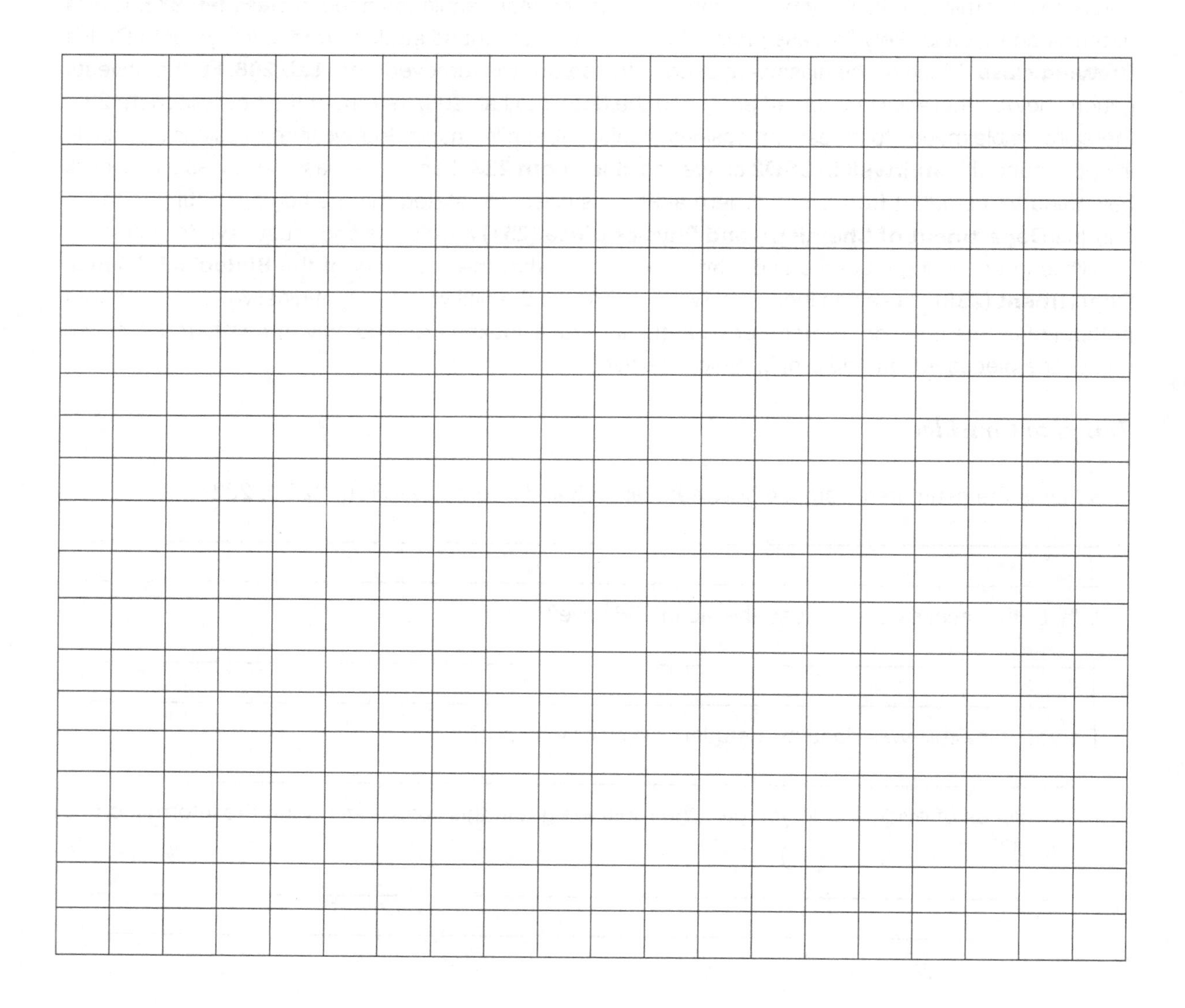

Crime Scene Summary Notes

The following summary notes are based on the lectures from Mr. Pycraft on crime scene investigation.

What type of crimes fall under the following categories:

Category One –

Category Two –

Category Three –

Seven-step crime scene protocol

1. Establish the __________ of the scene and identify potential ______ and ______________.
2. __________ the scene.
3. _______ and ________________ tasks and responsibilities.
4. Conduct a _____________________ to evaluate the probative value of potential crime scene processing activities.
5. ____________ and ______________ the scene and/or item(s) of potential evidence.
6. Conduct a ________________________ to complete a detailed examination of the scene.
7. ___________ and ______________ the evidence from the scene.

Crime scene search patterns

What is the purpose of a crime scene log?

How many entrances/exits should there be at a ***secured*** crime scene? __________

Important terms:

Crime scene log –

Entry/Exit –

Evidence –

Photography–

Overall photo –

Medium-range photo –

Close-up photo –

Additional Resources

Listed are materials for additional study specific to the area of crime scene investigation.

Robinson, E. (2010). *Crime Scene Photography* (2nd ed.). Elsevier Science &Technology Books.

Gardner, R. M. (2012). *Practical Crime Scene Processing and Investigation* (2nd ed.). CRC Press.

Fisher, B. and Fisher, D. (2012). *Techniques of Crime Scene Investigation*, (8th ed.). CRC Press.

CHAPTER THREE

Physical Evidence

Lab 3-1 Proper Packaging

OBJECTIVE Introduce students to the various ways evidence can be packaged.

DIRECTIONS: Examine the photos provided by your instructor. Determine the proper way to package the items.

Key notes:

- Drug items must be packaged in clear packaging.
- DNA items must be packaged in "breathable" packaging, such as paper bags or envelopes.
- All wet items should be dried before packaging.
- Unknown liquids/flammables/smelly items may need to be packaged in vials/paint cans/etc.

Photo number: ______________

Item: ________________________

How should the item be packaged? ____

Photo number: ______________

Item: ________________________

How should the item be packaged? ____

Photo number: ______________

Item: ________________________

How should the item be packaged? ____

Photo number: ______________

Item: ________________________

How should the item be packaged? ____

Photo number: ______________

Item: ________________________

How should the item be packaged? ____

Photo number: ____________

Item: ______________________

How should the item be packaged? ____

Photo number: ____________

Item: ______________________

How should the item be packaged? ____

Photo number: ____________

Item: ______________________

How should the item be packaged? ____

Photo number: ____________

Item: ______________________

How should the item be packaged? ____

Photo number: ____________

Item: ______________________

How should the item be packaged? ____

Photo number: ____________

Item: ______________________

How should the item be packaged? ____

Lab 3-2 Proper Markings and Seals

OBJECTIVE Introduce students to the markings that should be on evidence.

DIRECTIONS Exam the photos that follow. What things are missing from the evidence that has been packaged?

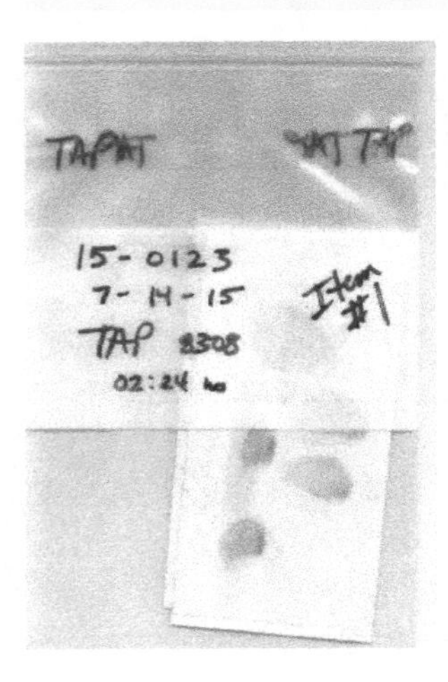

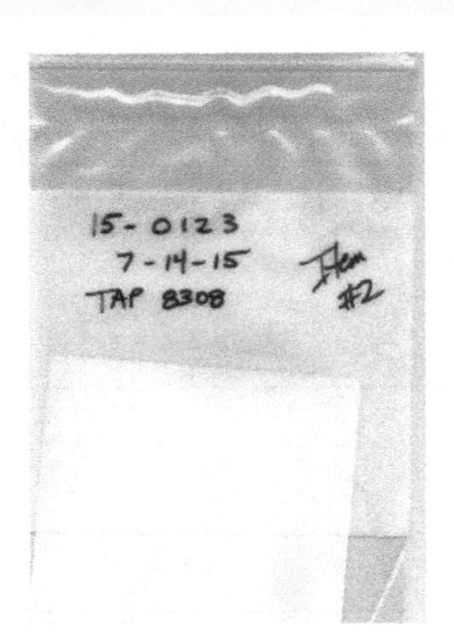

____

____

____

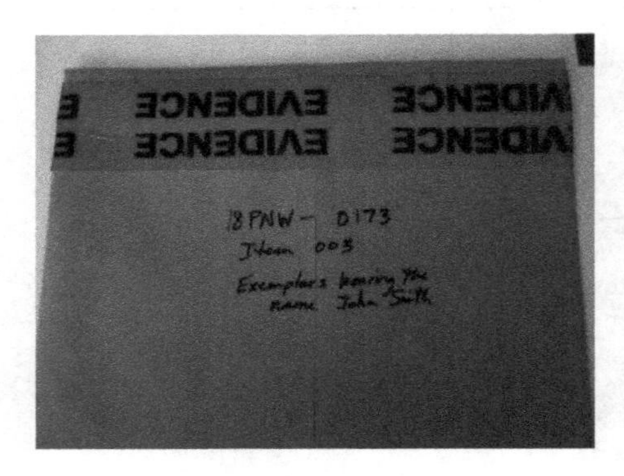

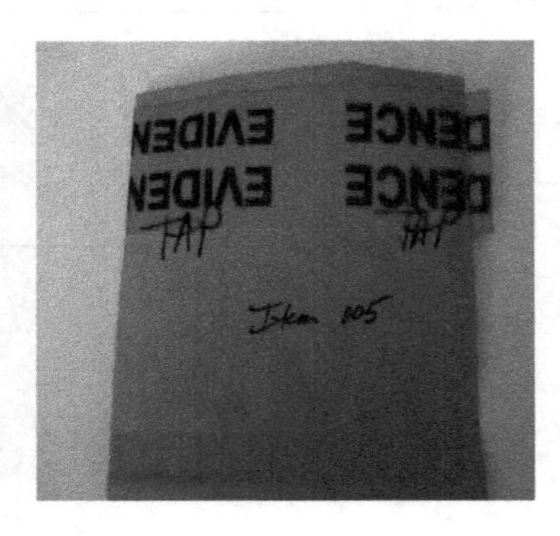

____

____

____

Lab 3-3 Laboratory Request

OBJECTIVE Introduce students to the various ways evidence can be packaged.

DIRECTIONS Complete the following tasks for the items in the list that follows:

A – Give which discipline(s) you would submit for laboratory examination

B – Explain how you would package the item

C –Think of possible questions you will need to ask the investigating officer

1. Bank robbery note

   A –

   B –

   C –

2. Pop can left at home burglary

   A –

   B –

   C –

3. Sweatshirt found in back alley of homicide

   A –

   B –

   C –

4. Cigarette butt found outside

   A –

   B –

   C –

5. Partially burned gas can with rag

   A –

   B –

   C –

6. Pair of shoes confiscated from suspect in burglary case

   A –

   B –

   C –

7. Pair of shoes confiscated from suspect in homicide case

   A –

   B –

   C –

8. Handgun confiscated from suspect vehicle

   A –

   B –

   C –

9. Handgun recovered from bottom of a retention pond

   A –

   B –

   C –

10. Bloody knife recovered from a crime scene

    A –

    B –

    C –

11. Unknown blue liquid recovered from possible meth lab

    A –

    B –

    C –

12. Small clear plastic baggie with plant material inside

    A –

    B –

    C –

13. Four, 9mm casings recovered at a crime scene

    A –

    B –

    C –

Evidence Summary Notes

The following summary notes are based on the lectures from Mr. Pycraft on evidence.

How can evidence be packaged?

__________ __________ __________

__________ __________ __________

____

What markings should be on the packaging of evidence?

1.
2.
3.
4.
5.

Why is masking tape an unacceptable type of tape for sealing evidence?

What is Locard's principal of exchange?

List three examples of biological evidence:

__________ __________ __________

List three examples of trace evidence:

__________ __________ __________

CHAPTER FOUR

Fingerprints

Lab 4-1 Classification

OBJECTIVE Introduce students to how fingerprints are classified.

DIRECTIONS Classify the latent prints as arch, loop, or whorl. Differentiate right slant loops from left slant loops.

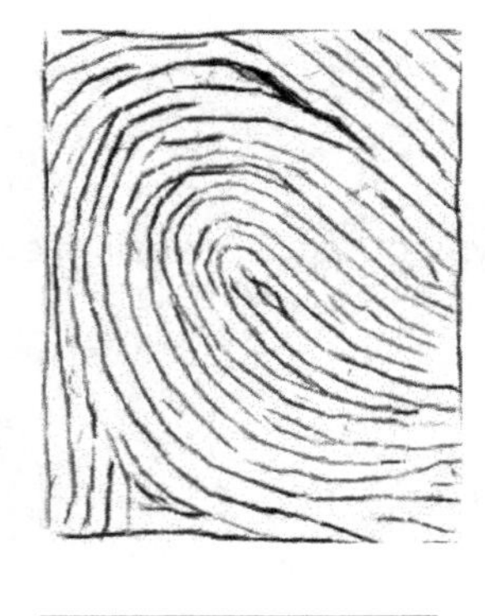

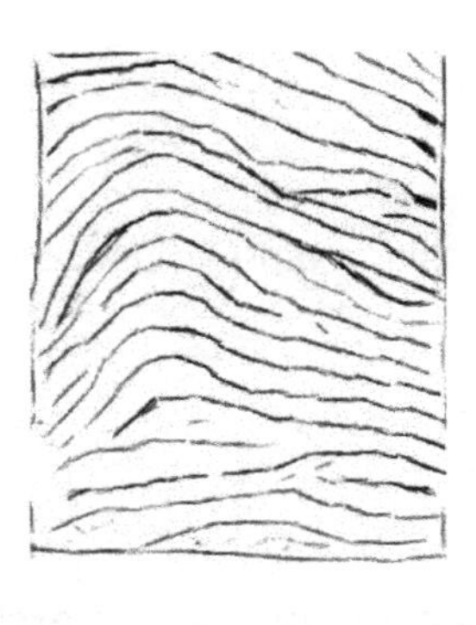

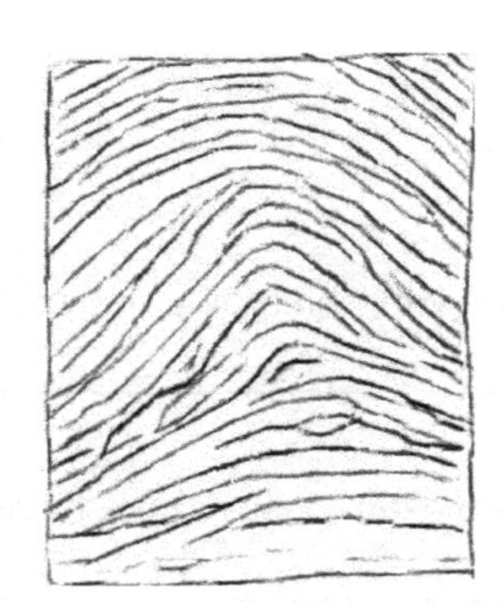

Lab 4-2 Following Ridge Paths

OBJECTIVE Introduce students to how analysts examine latent prints and the specific things they look for.

DIRECTIONS Trace the ridges with various colors of highlighters. Try to distinguish each ridge with a different color until you need to repeat colors.

Mark: Ridge endings—where a ridge stops **Bifurcations—where a ridge forks/splits**

Lab 4-3 Pattern Recognition

OBJECTIVE Test students' visual ability to recognize a pattern.

DIRECTIONS Which row contains the section of pattern from the left? Using a highlighter, mark the area(s).

nnnmnnnm

mnnmnnnmnmnnnmmnnnmmnnnmmnn

mnnnnnnnmnnnnnnnnnnnnnmmnnnnnn

mmmnmmmmnmmmnmmmmnmmmmmnmm

mnnnnnmnnnmnnnnnmnnmnnnmnnnm

llilllilli

lllilllllililiiiiliiiliiiliiiililiiiilllllliliiiliiliiliiliiiliiil

llliilllililllllilllilliliiiliilliiilllliliiilllilllililililili

llliillllillllilllilllllilllillllilllillllilllliilllliilllli

illlillililllillillilllilillilililliillilillilillilillililil

vwvwwvwv

wwwvwvwvwvwvwvwvwvwvwvwvwvwvwvvvvww

vvwwvvwwvvwwvvwwvvwwvvwwvvwwvvwwvv

wwwwvwwwvwwwvwwvwwwvwwwvwwwvwwwwwv

vwwwvvwwvwwwvwwwvvwwwvvwwwvvwwwvwv

Lab 4-4 Comparison

OBJECTIVE Introduce the concept of side-by-side comparisons.

DIRECTIONS Determine if the following impressions were made by the same source.

Circle your answer.

YES NO

What factors influenced your decision process?

____

____

Lab 4-5 What's of Value?

OBJECTIVE Teach students that just because you touch a surface, it doesn't mean that there is always an identifiable print.

DIRECTIONS Create your own fingerprint lifts off of various surfaces. Develop a key of your answers. Switch with another group and see how you do. Determine if the latent is of **value**. If so, **where** on the hand might the latent come from? (Optional: Examine the lifts provided by your instructor.)

Lift Pack #________

Lift 1

Value: ________

Location: ________

Lift 2

Value: ________

Location: ________

Lift 3

Value: ________

Location: ________

Lift 4

Value: ________

Location: ________

Lift 5

Value: ________

Location: ________

Lift 6

Value: ________

Location: ________

Lab 4-6 Friction Ridge Search

OBJECTIVE Allow students to engage in the comparison process and work on finding specific target groups.

DIRECTIONS Using highlighters, mark the positions of the six smaller boxes in the larger area of friction ridge skin.

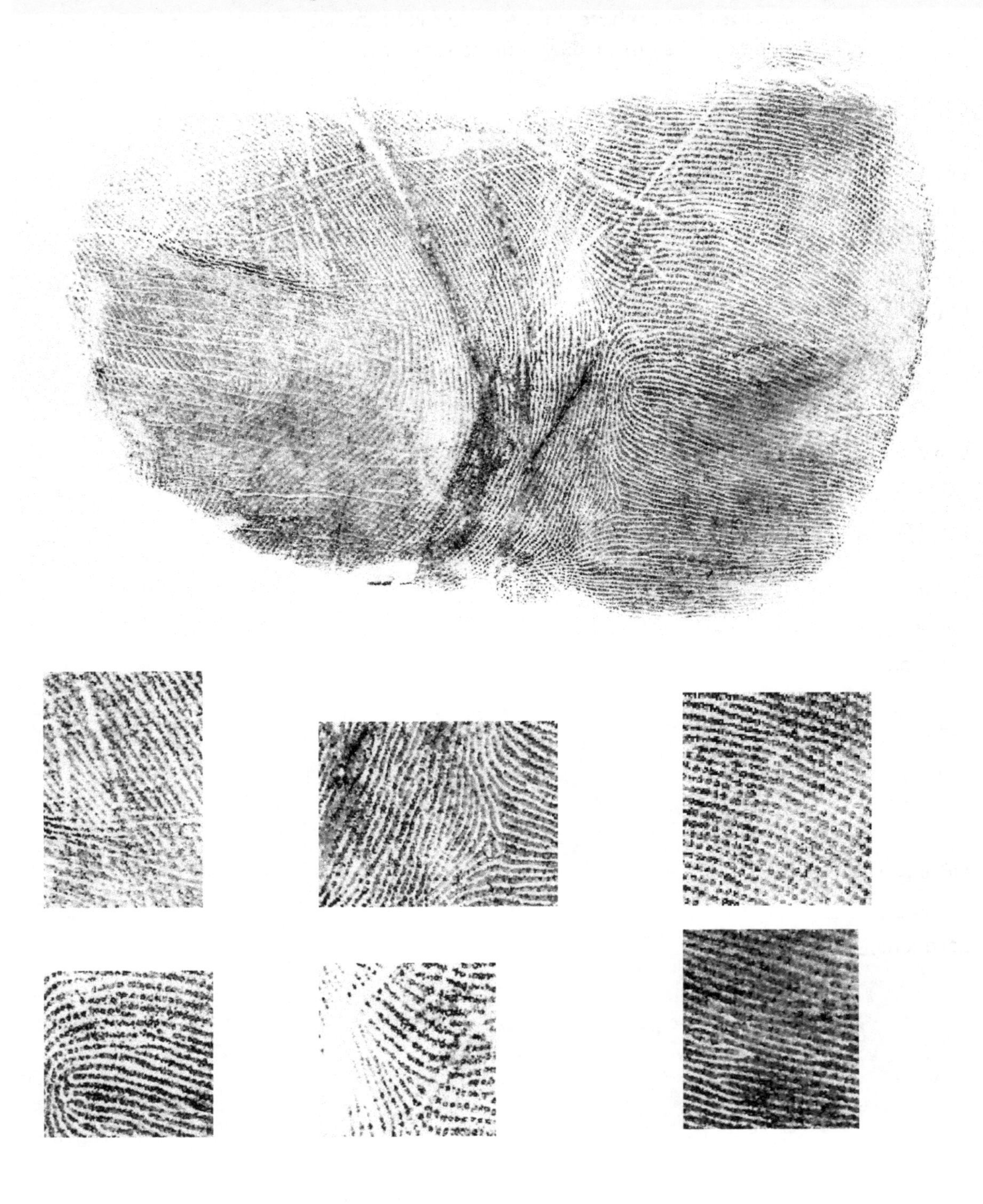

Study Guide Summary Notes

The following summary notes are based on the lectures from Mr. Pycraft on fingerprints.

What is friction ridge skin?

Where is it found?

When does it develop?

Between ________ and ________.

Injuries to the basal cells that reach the dermis layer will result in a ______________ __________.

Prior to 1903, an individual's identity was based primarily on ________________ measurements.

Define:

Latent print –

Patent print –

Plastic print –

The three main types of fingerprint patterns are

_________________, __________________, and _________________

What are the individual ridge characteristics that a forensic scientist looks for?

1. ______________________ 2. ___________________________

3. ______________________ 4. ___________________________

How many levels of **detail** is a forensic scientist looking for in a comparison?

____

Define:

Core –

Delta –

What does ACE+V stand for?

Additional Resources

Listed are materials for additional study specific to the area of fingerprints.

US Department of Justice (2011). *The Fingerprint Sourcebook*. National Institute of Justice.

Ashbaugh, D. (1999). *Quantitative—Qualitative Friction Ridge Analysis: An introduction to basic and advanced ridgeology*. CRC Press.

Ramtowski, R. (Ed.) (2013). *Advances in Fingerprint Technology* (3rd ed.). CRC Press.

Footwear / Tire Impressions

Lab 5-1 Impression Detail

OBJECTIVE Test students on perception/recognition of details in the tread.

DIRECTIONS Examine the images; try to determine the brand from the information within the tread design.

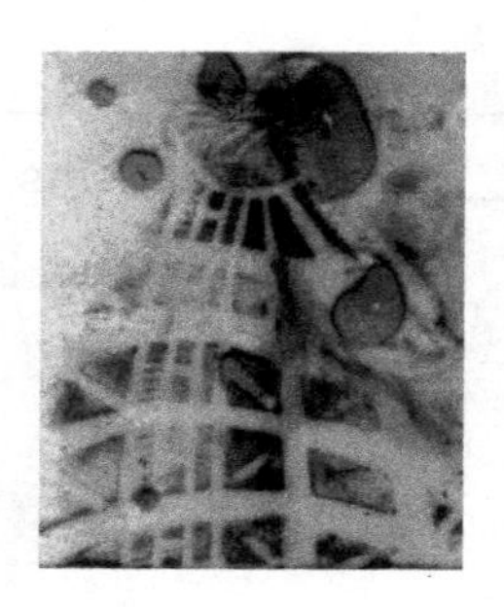

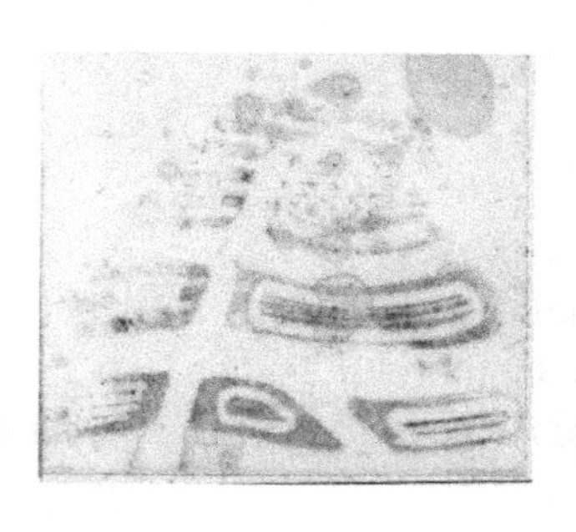

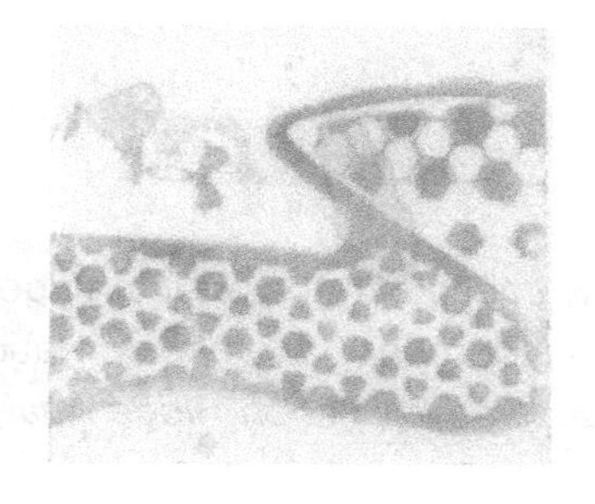

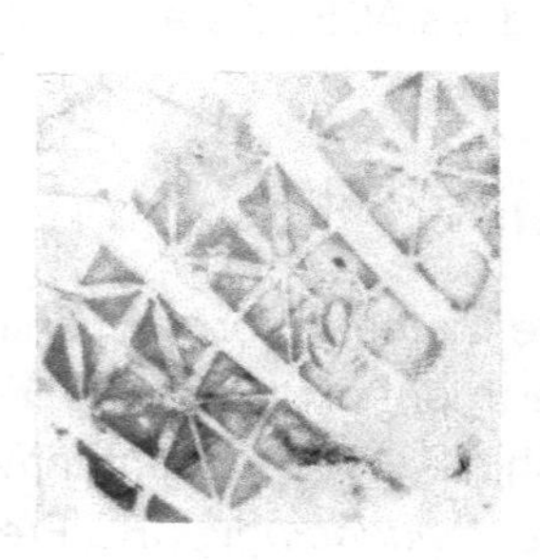

Lab 5-2 Class Characteristics vs Individual Characteristics

OBJECTIVE This lab differentiates class characteristics and individual characteristics, a major concept students will need to grasp during the exam of footwear.

DIRECTIONS Examine the photo. List the class characteristics below from the shoe. In the close-up photos circle the individualizing characteristics that make this shoe unique to all others of the same make/model/size.

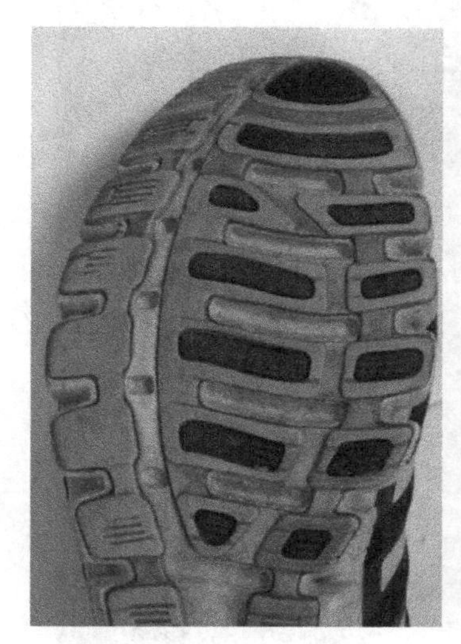

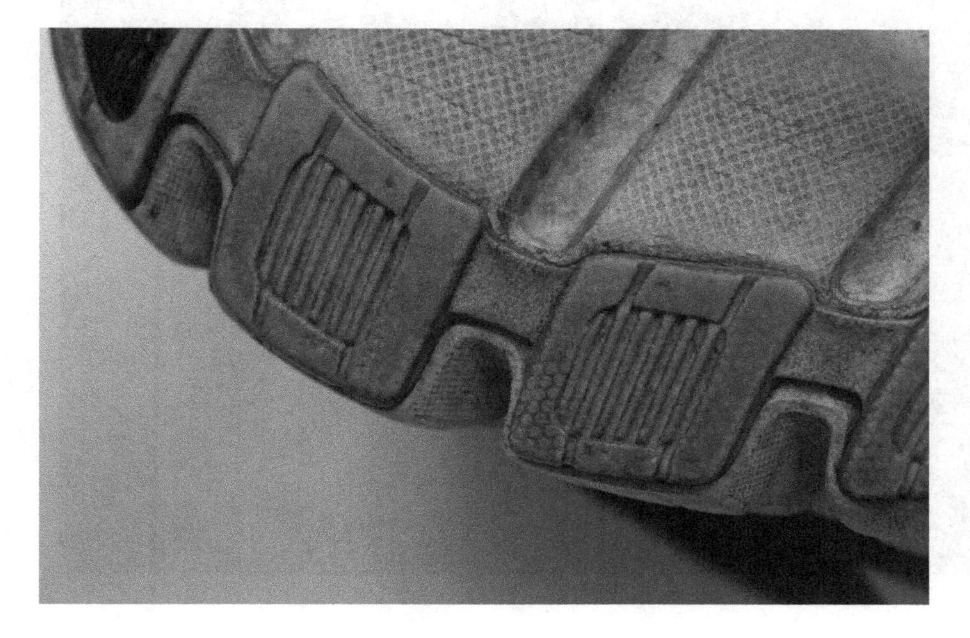

Class characteristics:

____

____

____

Examine the photo. List the class characteristics below. How would you differentiate between footwear impressions left from these two shoes?

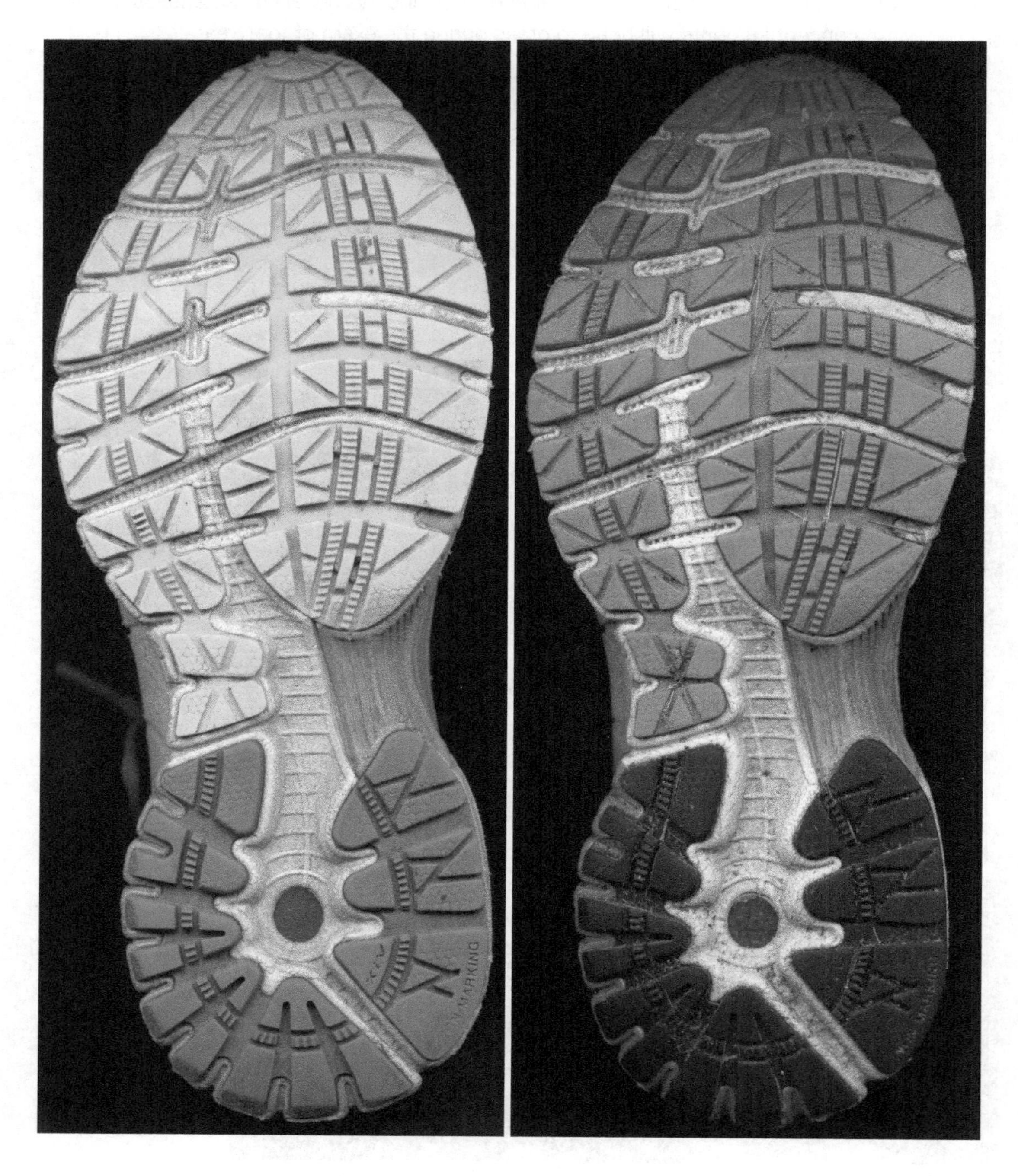

Class characteristics:

____

____

____

Examine the photo. List the class characteristics of the tires below. What do you notice about the pitch sequence?

Class characteristics:

____

____

____

Lab 5-3 Understanding 2-D Impressions

OBJECTIVE Introduce students to the examination process of footwear.

DIRECTIONS Examine the footwear impressions in the kit provided by your instructor. Answer the following.

Item #______

Can you determine the following?

How many impressions do you see in the lift?

What is the quality of the impression(s)? Clarity?

Can you determine the class characteristics? What are they?

Can you determine any accidental (individual) characteristics? What are they?

Can you determine the size of the shoe from the impression in the lift?

Can you distinguish between the right and the left shoe? Which do you think it is?

Lab 5-4 Making Exemplars

OBJECTIVE This exercise allows students to experience how exemplars are made. They are often used for comparison, in conjunction with the shoes submitted for comparison, to aide an analyst in what impression that shoe will actually make. Various surfaces can be used to help replicate the conditions with the footwear impression in question.

YOU WILL NEED Clear shoe polish or Vaseline, an applicator (or sponge), 8.5" X 14" paper, and magnetic fingerprint powder.

Directions:
1. Lay out several sheets of paper on the floor/carpet/mat.
2. Lightly apply shoe polish/Vaseline to the bottom of your shoe (or shoe you want to make an exemplar of).
3. Walk normally across the pieces of paper
4. Using magnetic fingerprint powder, apply powder over footwear impression.

These exemplars can also be used to make transparencies for comparison.

Lab 5-5 Casting

OBJECTIVE Allow students to experience how 3-D impressions are preserved.

DIRECTIONS Create a footwear/tire impression and use casting material to preserve the impression.

1. Create impression (This can be outside or in a small tray) [Dirt, fine mulch soil, sand, snow]
2. Photograph your impression with/without scale [90 degrees]
3. Use a casting frame – aluminum/poster board/cardstock
4. Mix dental stone in plastic bag (dental stone 2-2.5 lbs. +10-16 oz. water)
5. Pour gently into one area of impression allowing the dental stone to flow over the remaining impression.
6. Allow cast to set
7. Carefully lift stone out. Clean gently with water
8. Mark the back of the cast appropriately

Chapter 5 Footwear and Tires Summary Notes

The following summary notes are based on the lectures from Mr. Pycraft on footwear and tires.

What is a class characteristic? List examples.

What is an accidental (individual) characteristic? List examples.

Due to sizing issues, it is very important to make sure the scale is on _____________ _____________ _________________ as the impression.

What two ways are evidence of 3D impressions preserved?

What ways can a 2D impression be preserved?

What are the two types of molds used in tire manufacturing?

What does the "pitch sequence" try to eliminate?

What do the last four numbers of a DOT number tell you?

First two: ________________________

Last two: ________________________

CHAPTER SIX

Documents

Lab 6-1 Handwriting Examination

OBJECTIVE Experience what it is like to examine variations in how words are formed by different writers.

DIRECTIONS The word *forensics* has been documented 32 times on the next page. Examine the style of writing and determine which words are paired (come from the same source). Pay close attention to variations in slope, height ratio, letter spacing, and ending strokes.

Place the number of the accompanying pair on the given line. If you believe 1 and 32 are a pair, you would place a 32 on the line for 1 and a 1 on the line for 32 (1._32_ ; 32. _1_).

1.______	17.______
2.______	18.______
3.______	19.______
4.______	20.______
5.______	21.______
6.______	22.______
7.______	23.______
8.______	24.______
9.______	25.______
10.______	26.______
11.______	27.______
12.______	28.______
13.______	29.______
14.______	30.______
15.______	31.______
16.______	32.______

1. Forensics
2. Forensics
3. Forensics
4. forensics
5. Forensics
6. Forensics
7. Forensics
8. forensics
9. forensics
10. Forensics
11. forensics
12. Forensics
13. Foren sics
14. forensics
15. forensics
16. ForenSics
17. Forensics
18. forensics
19. Forensics
20. Forensics
21. Forensics
22. Forensics
23. forensics
24. forensics
25. Forensics
26. Forensics
27. forensics
28. forensics
29. Forensics
30. forensics
31. forensics
32. forensics

Lab 6-2 Note Examinations

OBJECTIVE Examine a questioned document for analysis and learn to detect variations that could be used when comparing to a known standard.

DIRECTIONS: Examine various notes provided by your instructor. Examine the style of writing. Use various highlighters to mark anything that stands out (grammar, spelling, word choice, handwriting, slant, spacing, height ratios, etc.) Answer the questions that follow

Note: __________

1. What jumps out at you in the note?

____

____

____

2. What does the length of the note tell you?

____

____

____

3. What consistencies do you notice in the note? Specific letters?

____

____

____

4. What inconsistencies do you notice in the note?

____

____

____

5. Can you determine the gender of the author? What supports your theory?

____

____

____

Note: ______________

1. What jumps out at you in the note?

____

____

____

2. What consistencies do you notice in the note? Specific letters?

____

____

____

3. What inconsistencies do you notice in the note?

____

____

____

Note: ______________

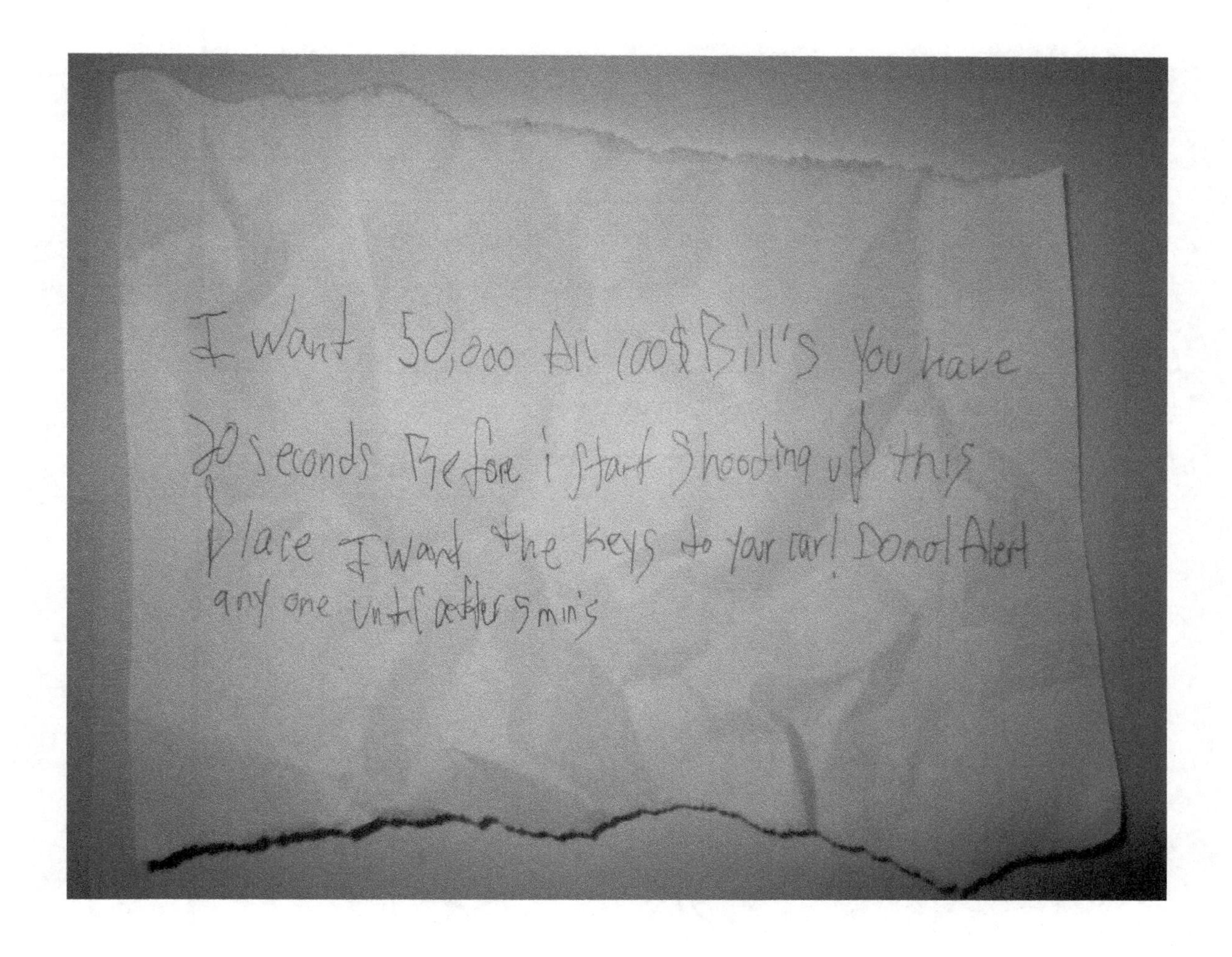
I want 50,000 All 100$ Bill's You have
20 seconds Before i start Shooding up this
place I want the keys to your car! Donot Alert
any one until after 5 min's

1. What jumps out at you in the note?

2. What consistencies do you notice in the note? Specific letters?

3. What inconsistencies do you notice in the note?

Note: ______________

Give Me All of Your
$ 50's & $ 100's Bills Now!!
OR Else!!

1. What jumps out at you in the note?

2. What consistencies do you notice in the note? Specific letters?

3. What inconsistencies do you notice in the note?

Lab 6-3 Ink Chromatography

OBJECTIVE Examine results from the separation of inks.

DIRECTIONS With a solvent provided by your instructor (acetone or isopropyl alcohol), fill the bottom of each test tube with a very small amount. On strips of filter paper, place a small line (horizontally) approximately 1 cm from the bottom. Place filter paper in test tube with solvent. Make sure solvent level is below the ink line.

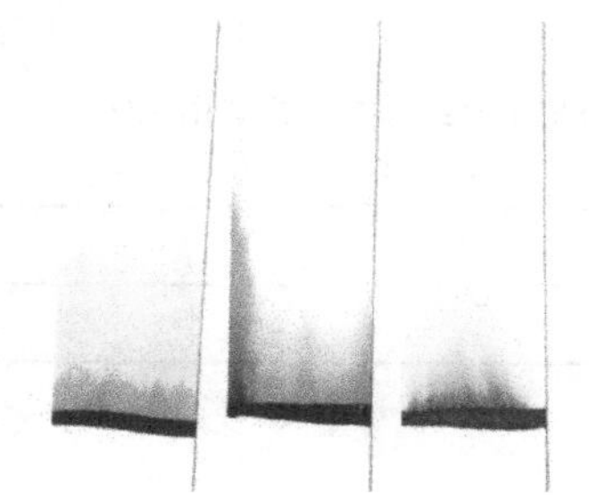

Ink color used: ____________________

Describe the chromatography results.

____

____

Ink color used: ____________________

Describe the chromatography results.

____

____

Study Guide Summary Notes

The following summary notes are based on the lectures from Mr. Pycraft on documents.

List some things that could be a questioned document?

In what areas might there be differences in handwriting?

__________________ __________________ __________________

__________________ __________________ __________________

__________________ __________________ __________________

What is an exemplar?

A suspect ______________ ______________ be shown the actual question document.

________________ illumination and photography can be used to reveal alterations, obliterations, and/or erasures.

Thin-layer chromatography can be used to __________________________ various ink dyes.

Terms you should recognize:

- Indented writings
- ESDA
- Alteration
- Obliteration
- Hesitation
- Counterfeiting

CHAPTER SEVEN

Firearms, Distance Determination, and Serial Number Restoration

Lab 7-1 Bullet Characterization

OBJECTIVE Expose students to the various class characteristics on a bullet.

DIRECTIONS Record the following information:

- Caliber
- Number of lands and grooves
- Direction of twist (right or left)
- Type of rifling (conventional or polygonal)
- Conclusion (exclusion or inconclusive)

Set #1 Number________

	Caliber	Number of Lands/Grooves	Twist	Rifling Type	Conclusion
A					
B					

Set #2 Number________

	Caliber	Number of Lands/Grooves	Twist	Rifling Type	Conclusion
A					
B					

Set #3 Number________

	Caliber	Number of Lands/Grooves	Twist	Rifling Type	Conclusion
A					
B					

Set #4 Number________

	Caliber	Number of Lands/Grooves	Twist	Rifling Type	Conclusion
A					
B					

Set #5 Number________

	Caliber	Number of Lands/Grooves	Twist	Rifling Type	Conclusion
A					
B					

Set #6 Number________

	Caliber	Number of Lands/Grooves	Twist	Rifling Type	Conclusion
A					
B					

Set ____ (A–E)

Bullet A

Caliber: ____________________

Bullet design: ____

Cannelures: Yes/No

Base: Flat/Concave Enclosed/Exposed

Bullet B

Caliber: ____________________

Bullet design: ____

Cannelures: Yes/No

Base: Flat/Concave Enclosed/Exposed

Bullet C

Caliber: ____________________

Bullet design: ____

Cannelures: Yes/No

Base: Flat/Concave Enclosed/Exposed

Bullet D

Caliber: ____________________

Bullet design: ____

Cannelures: Yes/No

Base: Flat/Concave Enclosed/Exposed

Bullet E

Caliber: ____________________

Bullet design: ____

Cannelures: Yes/No

Base: Flat/Concave Enclosed/Exposed

Lab 7-2 Distance Determination

OBJECTIVE Expose students to the various GSR patterns observed from different distances.

You will need the following:

- Five t-shirts that have gunshot residue patterns
- Five to seven standards (poster board) of known distance determinations

DIRECTIONS Assign the number of the clothing item to the correct distance from which the shot was fired.

Examine the shirts without use of the standards first.

Without standards

Contact ______

Two to four inches ______

Twelve inches ______

Four feet ______

Indeterminate _______

Now using the known standards, examine the patterns again. Do any of your answers change?

With Standards

Contact ______

Two to four inches ______

Twelve inches ______

Four feet ______

Indeterminate _______

Lab 7-3 Serial Number Restoration

OBJECTIVE Expose students to the process of serial number restoration.

You will need the following:

- A *serial number kit* with various small pieces of metal that have previously stamped numbers
- A *serial number restoration kit* with various reagents (Fry's reagent, Turner's reagent)
- A drummel or other tool that can sand metals
- A camera

DIRECTIONS Determine the type of metal you are dealing with (steel, lead, aluminum), because this will determine the reagents and acids you will use on them. Grind the area where the serial number was until it is smooth. Clean the area. Follow kit directions on specific metal.

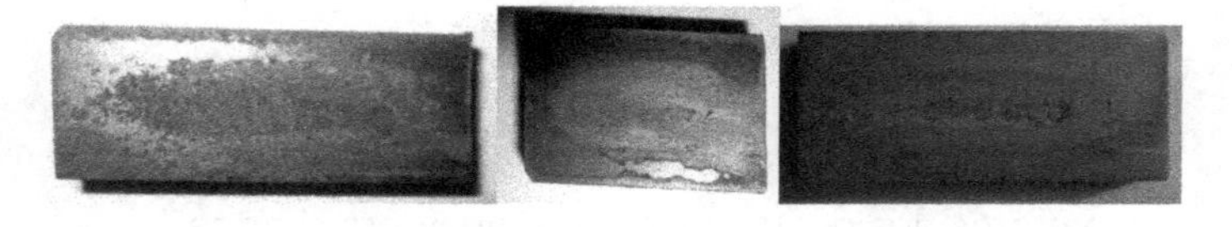

Results

____

____

____

Study Guide Summary Notes

The following summary notes are based on the lectures from Mr. Pycraft on firearms.

What is firearms identification?

Distinguish the differences between a pistol and a revolver and the differences between a rifle and a shotgun.

Pistol: Rifle:

Revolver: Shotgun:

What is the main piece of lab equipment used to examine microscopic identifying characteristics on ammunition?

Define the following terms: cartridge, cartridge case, and bullet.

What are examples of class characteristics (specific to the firearms discipline)?

________________ ________________ ________________

________________ ________________ ________________

________________ ________________ ________________

How does rifling influence a bullet's flight path?

The somewhat star-shaped pattern with triangular tears around a bullet hole made from a contact shot is called a ________________________.

The black ring made of oils and residues that is left around the initial entrance hole of a fired bullet is called a ________________________.

What does the NIBIN/IBIS database provide for investigators?

During chemical processing for distance determination, what chemical residues may be detected?

Terms you should recognize:

- Lands
- Grooves
- Caliber
- Gauge
- Powder patterns

CHAPTER EIGHT

Drugs

Lab 8-1 Drug Identification

OBJECTIVE Experience the process of analyzing controlled substances seen in casework.

You will need the following:

- Scenario packets
- Case-based info

DIRECTIONS Obtain an unknown (case-scenario packet) from your instructor.

Using the correct worksheet from the following pages, fill out the test results as if you had run those tests (visual, color tests, UV, TLC, FTIR, GC/MS).

Then, compare the results with the maintained drug monographs found at the Scientific Working Group for the Analysis of Seized Drugs (SWGDRUG, www.swgdrug.org) to determine which controlled substance or mixture is in your unknown.

Drug Examination Worksheet

Balance Calibration

Date:__________

Case Number:________________

Item Number:________________

Weight:________ net/gross

Balance used: ______________

Serial Number: ___________

Start date/End date: ____/_____

UOM: ________

Date performed: ______ Blanks:_____

Marquis: ____________________________

p-DMAB: ____________________________

Dille-KoppanyiL ______________________

Cobalt Thiocyanate____________________

Mecke's: ____________________________

Sodium nitroprusside: _________________

Other: ______________________________

UV: ____

Preparation:

____

____

Solvent: ___________

Filtered: ___________

Date performed: ________________

TLC: __________________________

Blank: _____ MeOH : NH4OH: ________________________

Blank: _____ CHCL3 : MeOH: HOAc: ________________________

Blank: _____ Other: _________________________

FTIR: (ATR): ____

Blank: __________

GC/MS: _____________________________________

Plant Material Examination Worksheet

Item: _________ Gross weight: ______ Net: _______ UOM: __________

Balance calibration: ____________

Case number: _________________

Date: __________

Item number: _________________

Balance used: ______________

Serial Number: ____________

Start date/End date: _____/______

Date performed: ________________

Microscopic: Cystolithic hairs ____________ Fine hairs ____________ Seeds ____________

Stems: ____________ Flowering tops ____________ Vein/Other ____________

Preparation: Petroleum ether rinse __________ $CHCL_3$ Rinse ___________ Other ___________

Date performed: ________________

Duquenois-Levine: ____ Blank: ________

Date performed: ________________

TLC: Toluene/Fast blue BB: ___________________________________ Blank: ________

Date performed: ________________

GC/MS: ____

____

Retention time: ____

____

Blank: __________

Tablets Examination Worksheet

Balance calibration: __________ Case number: ______________

Date: __________ Item number: ______________

Sampled: ________ net/gross

Balance used: ____________

Serial Number: __________

Start date/End date: _____/_____

UOM: ________

Not analyzed: ___________ net/gross

UOM: _______

Active ingredient(s): ____________________

____

Control status: ____________________

MFR/Trade name: ________________

Reference: ____________________

UV: ______________________________

Preparation: ____

____

Solvent: __________

Filtered: __________

Date performed: ______________

TLC: ____________________

Blank: _____ MeOH: NH4OH: ____________________

Blank: _____ CHCL3: MeOH: HOAc: ____________________

Blank: _____ Other: ____________________

FTIR: (ATR): ____

Blank:__________

GC/MS: ____

____

Study Guide Summary Notes

The following summary notes are based on the lectures from Mr. Pycraft on drugs.

What does HIDTA stand for?

What are some major types of drugs?

__________________ __________________ __________________ __________________

__________________ __________________

Drugs are categorized into __________________ of classification based on a drug's potential for __________, potential for __________, and ______ value.

Differentiate between a qualitative test and a quantitative test.

A synthetic opiate used to treat people who are addicted to opiate based drugs is called _____________.

MDMA is the abbreviation for the drug known on the street as _____________.

Most of the world's heroin originates in this region: _________________________.

Ephedrine is the single most important ingredient in the manufacturing of the street drug ________________.

CHAPTER NINE

Trace

Lab 9-1 Fracture Match—Tape

OBJECTIVE Allow students to examine torn tape.

You will need the following:

- Torn pieces of duct tape (It is recommended to place them on clear transparency and then trim around the tape.)

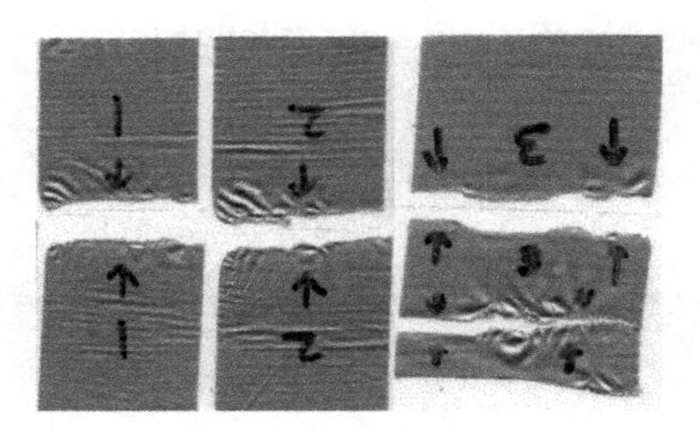

In this lab, you will be asked to determine if the sections of tape go together. Determine which ends go together and write your answers in the spaces provided. You must complete two tape groups. Each tape group will have four sections that match.

Tape group: ____________________

MATCHING ENDS

____________________ to ____________________
____________________ to ____________________
____________________ to ____________________
____________________ to ____________________

Tape group: ____________________

MATCHING ENDS

____________________ to ____________________
____________________ to ____________________
____________________ to ____________________
____________________ to ____________________

Lab 9-2 Fracture Match—Plastic

OBJECTIVE Allow students to examine broken plastic.

You will need the following:

- Broken pieces of plastic that can be pieced back together (Broken turn signal, broken piece of bumper, etc.)

Scenario:
You are a member of the Trace Unit. You have been assigned a case involving a hit and run. This case is a homicide since the victim passed away from his or her injuries at the hospital. Witnesses at the scene were able to describe the suspect vehicle. At the scene, pieces of a broken turn signal (Item 001) were collected by the CSI. Weeks later, a suspect was developed after a tip came in from an auto body shop. The broken turn signal (Item 015) was retrieved and submitted for examination.

Examine Items 001 and 015.

Does Item 001 match the turn signal from Item 015? Give reasons to support your answer.

____

____

____

CHAPTER TEN

Biology

Lab 10-1 Presumptive Testing

OBJECTIVE Experience testing suspected blood stains with presumptive tests.

DIRECTIONS There are three unknowns prepared for your testing. Using a sterile swab or testing strip (Hemastix **R**/Sero-testsTM) determine if the sample contains blood. Indicate the color change that occurred. List your findings in the spaces provided.

Examples:

- Positive phenolphthalein: No reaction
- Slow color change
- Pink/yellow to blue-green

Step I: Transfer a small amount of unknown onto a sterile swab
Step II: Add 1 drop of phenolphthalein solution
Step III: Add 1 drop of hydrogen peroxide

Sample A

____

Sample B

____

Sample C

____

Discussion Questions
Did you have any negative tests? ______________________________
Do you think any of the positive tests might be a *false* positive? ______________________________

Lab 10-2 A Clean-Up or False Positive

OBJECTIVE Experience how CSIs find potential areas where blood has been cleaned up or wiped away.

You will need the following:

- Training blood
- Non-bleach cleaner
- Bleach-based cleaner
- Luminol or Bluestar

DIRECTIONS On a counter top, table, or sink area, create a bloody crime scene (using synthetic training blood). Grid the area into three or four sections. Each area will be cleaned up with a different method.

Area 1

Non-bleach cleaner

Area 2

Bleach based cleaner

Area 3

Water only

Area 4 (optional)

Optional cleaner/diluted bleach

After the cleaning is done, turn out the lights and use Luminol/Bluestar. Record results.

____

____

____

____

Lab 10-3 Bloodstain Pattern Analysis (BPA)

With crime scenes, it is not uncommon to be called to a scene that involves bloodstains. Being able to interpret what happened depends on understanding certain things about the blood patterns.

Direction of impact, angle of impact, area of origin, where was the victim, where was the suspect, etc.—these all have their way of giving an investigator the clues he or she needs.

In your group complete the following:

1. How does *height* change the appearance of a blood droplet?

   ____

   ____

   ____

   Using the pipet and spatter blood, release a single drop of blood from different heights onto butcher paper.

Use a measuring tape/scale. Record the size (width and length), shape, and tails.

1 ft. Result ____________________

__ ft. Result ____________________

__ft. Result ____________________

__ft. Result ____________________

8 ft. Result ____________________

2. How does *horizontal* motion change the appearance of a blood droplet?

____

____

____

Using the pipet and spatter blood, release drops of blood as you move (walk versus run) along the butcher paper. Record your results.

What does a *tail* in blood drops indicate? ____________________

3. How does *angle of impact* change the appearance of a blood droplet?
Using the pipet and cardboard, release a single drop of blood from different angles

15 degrees Result ____________________

30 degrees Result ____________________

45 degrees Result ____________________

90 degrees Result ____________________

4. How does *surface* change the appearance of a blood droplet (linoleum, tile, carpet, sidewalk). Record the size, shape, circumference, and diameter.

____

____

____

1 ft. Result ____________________

5 ft. Result ____________________

5. How far does blood travel on the bottom of your shoe? Using a role of butcher paper, make a small pool of blood (size of a quarter). Have a student step in the blood and continue to walk until the blood is no longer detected. Record your results.

____

____

____

What was the distance you could still identify the shoe pattern? ____________________

Lab 10-4 DNA Profiles

OBJECTIVE Experience how a DNA analyst compares profiles that were generated from samples in casework.

DIRECTIONS In the scenario provided, examine the profile developed (single contributor or mixture) in the case and compare to the profiles submitted for comparison (STR summary sheet).

Scenario A Case Number: 103246

At a residential burglary, the suspect is believed to have entered the home through a broken window. During processing of the scene, the CSI found a reddish-brown stain on some of the pieces of glass that potentially could be blood. The stains were swabbed and packaged for processing at the forensic laboratory. DNA was run on Item #3, and a profile was obtained. A victim elimination standard, as well as a possible suspect standard, were also submitted to the lab. Examine the single Contributor data sheet and the STR summary sheet. Answer the following questions.

- Who is the source of the single contributor profile?____________________
- What is the statistical probability that a random African American/Caucasian/Hispanic would have the same alleles detected?
    - African American __________
    - Caucasian __________
    - Hispanic __________
- At which locations (if any) did the victim and suspect share similarities in their profiles?

When dealing with DNA stats, there is potential to be dealing with extremely large numbers. When expressing this information to a jury, you may get a look of disbelief and/or confusion; however, these are real numbers.

How many zeroes are in the following:

Septillion: _______ Nonillion: _______ Undecillion: _______ Tredecillion: _______

Single Contributor

Random Match Probablity

Case Number	103426
Item Number	3
Analyst	Joe Smith
Date	

Alleles Detected	
VWZ	X, Y
AS7G431	11, 19
AS13G25	14, 20.3
AS6G8	10, 17
AS10G327	9, 15
AS4G94	12, 13
Delta P	8
AS18G692	8, 13
AS3G745	21
AS11G86	19, 21
UCF9R	4, 15
Delta F	4, 11
CH16	5, 8
vUM	17, 19
AS23G10	31, 36
AS5G334	6, 14
AS2G851	12, 18
JTEC	9, 15
AS8G1214	10, 16
AS14G377	13, 25
AS18G65	9, 17
GC22	18.2
AS25G17	16, 20
ASY261	7, 12
INT	18, 22
ASY873	19, 21
ASY914	21, 24

			African American		**Caucasian**		**Hispanic**	
VWZ								
AS7G431	11	19	0.0190	0.0190	0.1276	0.1735	0.0120	0.0144
AS13G25	14	20.3	0.0140	0.0119	0.1404	0.0123	0.1788	0.0120
AS6G8	10	17	0.0698	0.2905	0.0150	0.0361	0.1986	0.0335
AS10G327	9	5	0.0335	0.0119	0.0124	0.0933	0.3238	0.0639
AS4G94	12	13	0.0140	0.4405	0.0123	0.1899	0.2048	0.0639
Delta P	8	8	0.0180	0.0119	0.1582	0.1788	0.1818	0.0215
AS18G692	8	13	0.0363	0.0143	0.0128	0.0639	0.1083	0.0139
AS3G745	21	21	0.0615	0.0335	0.2537	0.0672	0.210S	0.0361
AS11G86	19	21	0.2150	0.0114	0.1122	0.1899	0.1083	0.0119
UCF9R	4	15	0.1788	0.1899	0.2219	0.1083	0.0933	0.0150
Delta F	4	11	0.0190	0.0583	0.0128	0.0129	0.0639	0.0722
CH16	5	8	0.1889	0.0139	0.3005	0.0335	0.0114	0.1788
vUM	17	19	0.0639	0.1636	0.0148	0.1899	0.1731	0.0639
AS23G10	31	36	0.0139	0.0471	0.1404	0.0143	0.2869	0.0124
AS5G334	6	14	0.1316	0.0180	0.1658	0.1788	0.0361	0.5470
AS2G851	12	18	0.0139	0.0639	0.2321	0.1083	0.1757	0.0335
JTEC	9	15	0.2238	0.0139	0.0550	0.0933	0.0114	0.1899
AS8G1214	10	16	0.0139	0.1788	0.0124	0.3168	0.2181	0.0987
AS14G377	13	25	0.0361	0.1986	0.1788	0.0639	0.0046	0.0143
AS18G65	9	17	0.0119	0.3238	0.0957	0.0129	0.3005	0.1083
GC22	18.2	18.2	0.0150	0.2048	0.1899	0.2334	0.0361	0.1788
AS25G17	16	20	0.0722	0.1818	0.0114	0.1807	0.2525	0.2802
ASY261	7	12	0.0139	0.0224	0.0335	0.1083	0.0718	0.0639
INT	18	22	0.2220	0.0129	0.3158	0.0143	0.2105	0.0672
ASY873	19	21	0.1083	0.0933	0.1788	0.1848	0.0114	0.0933
ASY914	21	24	0.0180	0.0139	0.3100	0.0129	0.0335	0.0120

Total African Am.	1.22E-40	5.3E+39	1 in	5.3	DUODECILLION
Total Caucasian	3.40E-39	1.7E+38	1 in	170	UNDECILLION
Total Hispanic	5.90E-41	4.5E+40	1 in	45	DUODECILLION

Controls Passed:	JS	Positive Control	Reagent Blank
Initials:	JS	Amp Blank	

STR Summary Sheet

Standards/Single Sources

Case number	103426
Analyst	Joe Smith
Date	

Sample	1	2				
Description	Victim	Suspect				
VWZ	X	X, Y				
AS7G431	15, 16	11, 19				
AS13G25	11,14	14, 20.3				
AS6G8	12	10, 17				
AS10G327	8, 13	9, 15				
AS4G94	7,10	12, 13				
Delta P	19, 21	8				
AS18G692	5, 15	8, 13				
AS3G745	15	21				
AS11G86	12, 26	19, 21				
UCF9R	7, 10	4,15				
Delta F	9, 11	4,11				
CH16	3, 10	5, 8				
vUM	16, 20	17, 19				
AS23G10	35	31, 36				
AS5G334	6, 16	6, 14				
AS2G851	4, 12	12, 18				
JTEC	13, 15	9, 15				
AS8G1214	7, 18	10, 16				
AS14G377	20, 24	13, 25				
AS18G65	13, 16	9, 17				
GC22	20, 30	18.2				
AS25G17	14, 19	16, 20				
ASY261		7, 12				
INT	19, 24	18, 22				
ASY873		19, 21				
ASY914		21, 24				

Controls Passed: JS Positive control Reagent blank

Initials: JS Amp blank

Scenario B Case Number: 18-002796

After a bar fight, two individuals (both male) continued their argument outside in the parking lot. At some point, one of the individuals was stabbed during the altercation. The victim was taken to the hospital in serious but stable condition. Numerous individuals were questioned by police, and one male was taken into custody. A knife (Item 012) was collected from the crime scene and was sent to the lab for testing.

In the lab, the knife was swabbed (Item 012 A) on the handle end, in order to attempt to develop a potential "handler" profile.

Examine the two contributor mixture data sheet and the STR summary sheet. Answer the following questions.

- Who is the source of the major profile in the Two Contributor Mixture? ________
- Who is the source of the minor profile in the Two Contributor Mixture? ________
- What are some of the reasons this item may have contained a mixture?

Two Contributor Mixture

Major/Minor Profile

Case Number	18-002796
Item Number	Item 012 A
Analyst	M. Stevens
Date	

	Mixture Alleles	Major		Minor	
		X	Y	X	Y
VWZ	X, Y	X	Y	X	Y
AS7G431	9, 12, 16, 20	9	20	12	16
AS13G25	13, 15, 16, 18.3	15	16	13	18.3
AS6G8	8, 11, 14, 17	11	17	8	14
AS10G327	12, 13, 18, 19	12	13	18	19
AS4G94	6, 10, 11, 17	10	17	6	11
Delta P	9, 15, 20, 24	9	24	15	20
AS18G692	4, 12	4	12	Masked	
AS3G745	11, 17, 23, 27	11	17	23	27
AS11G86	12, 15	*	*	*	*
UCF9R	5, 7, 13	5	13	7	M
Delta F	2.2, 9, 12, 16	2.2	16	9	12
CH16	10	10	10	*	*
vUM	14, 15, 21, 22	15	22	14	21
AS23G10	26, 29, 30, 34	29	30	26	34
AS5G334	6, 13, 16	6	13	13	16
AS2G851	9, 12, 15, 18	15	18	9	12
JTEC	4, 7, 11, 16	7	16	4	11
AS8G1214	8, 14, 17, 19	14	17	8	19
AS14G377	15, 20, 23, 26	15	20	23	26
AS18G65	5.2, 10, 16, 18	5.2	18	10	16
GC22	13, 19	13	19	Masked	
AS25G17	7, 9, 15, 17	9	17	7	15
ASY261	10, 11	10		*	*
INT	14, 20, 22, 23	14	22	20	23
ASY873	16, 18	16		13	21
ASY914	10, 21	10	21	10	*

Controls Passed: MS Positive Control Reagent Blank

Initials: MS Amp Blank

STR Summary Sheet
Standards/Single Sources

Case number	18-002796
Analyst	M. Stevens
Date	

Sample	1	2				
Description	Victim	Suspect				
VWZ	X, Y	X, Y				
AS7G431	12, 16	9, 20				
AS13G25	13, 18.3	15, 16				
AS6G8	8, 14	11, 17				
AS10G327	18,19	12, 13				
AS4G94	6, 11	10, 17				
Delta P	15, 20	9, 24				
AS18G692	10, 12	4, 12				
AS3G745	23, 27	11, 17				
AS11G86	17, 19	12, 15				
UCF9R	7	5, 13				
Delta F	9, 12	2.2, 16				
CH16	6, 9	10				
vUM	14, 21	15, 22				
AS23G10	26, 34	29, 30				
AS5G334	13, 16	6, 13				
AS2G851	9, 12	15, 18				
JTEC	4, 11	7, 16				
AS8G1214	8, 19	14, 17				
AS14G377	23, 26	15, 20				
AS18G65	10, 16	5.2, 18				
GC22	17, 20	13, 19				
AS25G17	7, 15	9, 17				
ASY261	12, 16	10, 11				
INT	20, 23	14, 22				
ASY873	13, 21	16, 18				
ASY914	10	10, 21				

Controls Passed: MS Positive control Reagent blank
Initials: MS Amp blank

Scenario C Case Number: PNW-03198

After a night out, a female has reported a sexual assault to police. While the details of the evening are fuzzy, she recalls going out with a group of friends. However, they met up with several individuals with whom she was not familiar. She recalls a few of the bars where they spent time but cannot remember how she got home to her apartment.

Her friends are interviewed, all feeling less than their best after an entertaining evening and a sobering phone call from investigators. They give additional details from the evening and mention that she "took a liking to Bobby," a regular at one of the bars.

Numerous items have been submitted to the lab. A sexual assault kit obtained from the victim, her clothing, as well as bedding from her apartment. Standards were collected and submitted from the victim and from the individual named Bobby.

Examine the two contributor mixture data sheet and the STR summary sheet. Answer the following questions.

- Who is the source of the major profile in the two contributor mixture?____________________________
- Who is the source of the minor profile in the two contributor mixture?____________________________

Two Contributor Mixture
Major/Minor Profile

Case Number	PNW-03198
Item Number	Item 21 A
Analyst	H. Rodriquez
Date	

	Mixture Alleles	Major		Minor	
VWZ	X Y	X	Y	X	
AS7G431	10, 14, 17, 20	10	17	14	20
AS13G25	15, 16, 19	16	19	15	16
AS6G8	11, 12, 13, 14	12	14	11	13
AS10G327	9, 15, 18	9	18	15	15
AS4G94	8, 9, 13	9	13	8	*
Delta P	6, 11, 12, 24	11	12	6	24
AS18G692	5, 6, 9, 11	5	6	9	11
AS3G745	8, 14.2, 23, 27	8	27	14.2	23
AS11G86	16, 17, 21, 26	17	21	16	26
UCF9R	7, 8, 10, 12	7	12	8	10
Delta F	3.2, 9, 20	9	20	3.2	3.2
CH16	4, 6, 7, 11	6	11	4	7
vUM	13, 15, 19, 21	13	21	15	19
AS23G10	26, 28, 35, 36	26	36	28	35
AS5G334	6, 11, 15	15	15	6	11
AS2G851	8, 9, 16, 18	9	16	8	18
JTEC	5, 8	5	8	*	*
AS8G1214	7, 10, 15	7	10	15	A
AS14G377	14, 16, 21	14	*	16	21
AS18G65	5.2, 12.5, 15, 18	5.2	15	12.2	18
GC22	4.2, 30, 37, 39	4.2	39	30	37
AS25G17	10, 12, 16, 20	12	20	10	16
ASY261	14	14			
INT	15, 17, 22, 23	15	23	17	22
ASY873	16	16			
ASY914	10	10			

Controls Passed: HR Positive Control Reagent Blank
Initials: HR Amp Blank

STR Summary Sheet
Standards/Single Sources

Case Number	PNW-03198
Analyst	H. Rodriquez
Date	

Sample	1	2				
Description	Victim	Suspect				
VWZ	X	X, Y				
AS7G431	14, 20	15, 18				
AS13G25	15, 16	9, 18.3				
AS6G8	11, 13	10, 16				
AS10G327	15	12, 17				
AS4G94	8, 17	5, 11				
Delta P	6, 24	8, 21				
AS18G692	9, 11	10, 12				
AS3G745	14.2, 23	17, 25				
AS11G86	16, 26	14, 22				
UCF9R	8, 10	9, 13				
Delta F	3.2	8, 11				
CH16	4, 7	3, 10				
vUM	15, 19	12, 24				
AS23G10	28, 35	27, 32				
AS5G334	6, 11	5, 15				
AS2G851	8, 18	13, 17				
JTEC	10, 14	10, 16				
AS8G1214	15, 19	11, 18				
AS14G377	16, 21	17, 26				
AS18G65	12.2, 18	9, 17				
GC22	30, 37	27, 34				
AS25G17	10, 16	10, 15				
ASY261		10, 11				
INT	17, 22	14, 50.2				
ASY873		15				
ASY914		11				

Controls Passed: HR   Positive Control   Reagent Blank
Initials: HR   Amp Blank

Study Guide Summary Notes

The following summary notes are based on the lectures from Mr. Pycraft on bloodstain pattern analysis.

The flight of a blood droplet is ____________ by the laws of physics.

A drop of blood keeps the form of a ____________ during flight due to ____________ ____________.

BPA is accepted in court because the patterns are ____________.

What are the *three* categories of bloodstains?

____________________ ____________________ ____________________

Define area of origin:

Define area of convergence:

How is angle of impact calculated?

What is cast-off bloodstaining?

What other patterns might be found at a crime scene?

______________ ______________ ______________ ______________

Additional Resources

Listed are materials for additional study specific to the area of BPA.

James, S., Kish, P., & Sutton, T. P. (2005). *Principles of bloodstain pattern analysis: Theory and practice.* CRC Press.

DiMaio, D. (2006). *Handbook of forensic pathology* (2nd ed.). CRC Press.

Gardner, R. (2012). *Practical crime scene analysis and reconstruction* (2nd ed.). CRC Press.

CHAPTER ELEVEN

The Mock—Putting It All Together

Lab 11-1 Outdoors

OBJECTIVE Work together as a team and complete a major scene. This lab encompasses many of the disciplines that have been covered in class and the techniques that have been learned.

DIRECTIONS Divide the class into groups of 10 to 12. There are many different jobs to accomplish.

Mock Crime Scene

Case # PNW-120417

You have been called to the scene of an attempted murder and attempted carjacking. The address is 2200 169th Street, Hammond, Indiana (GYTE parking lot). The officer in charge is Lieutenant Michael Brown from the Indiana State Police Criminal Investigation division.

The victim, Sarah Jones (white, female, 25 years old), has been transported to St. Margaret Mercy Hospital in Hammond, Indiana with multiple gun-shot wounds (left forearm and left abdomen). She is listed in critical but stable condition.

Witnesses reported that two masked individuals, possibly white males, approached Jones's car as she prepared to exit her car. One suspect opened the driver's door and struggled with Jones. The other suspect entered Jones's car through the front passenger's door and was pushing Jones out of the car. During the struggle, the suspect at the driver's door fired multiple shots from a black pistol. Jones was struck. The suspects removed Jones from the vehicle and attempted to steal the vehicle. They could not get the vehicle started. Witnesses further reported that the suspects fled the scene eastbound, on foot, out of sight, prior to uniformed law enforcement personnel arriving.

Emergency medical personnel arrived, stabilized Jones, and then transported her to the hospital.

There is an active manhunt underway for the suspects that are at large. A possible footwear impression was found in the direction witnesses stated the suspects fled.

For the purpose of your reporting documents, use today's date and current time. The actual time of the incident was 2:55 p.m.

Mock Crime Scene

Team: __________
Team leader: ________________________
Crime scene log:______________________
Photography unit:____
Sketch team:____
Evidence team: ____
Lifting and pouring: ____
Additional paperwork: ____

Your team must complete the following:

- Establish who will do each job.
- Establish a crime scene log for who enters and exits the scene.
- Photograph the scene (360 degrees): overall photos, all evidence, close-ups with scale. Complete photo log.
- Sketch the crime scene. This team will be responsible for measurements of the scene as well.
- "Collect" the evidence from the scene (don't actually take it out of the scene as other groups are still working). Seal packaging in proper evidence type (envelope, paper bag, plastic, can, etc.).
- Fingerprint the "marked area" (associated to your group number). Lift *all* latents in that area with tape lifters, place on backers, and fill out information.
- Pour a cast of suspect shoe impression.

CRIME SCENE LOG

All personnel *must* sign before entering the crime scene.

Scene location: ______________________

Date: _______________

Agency:_____________________

Agency case number:_____________

Name/Rank	Agency	Initials	Time In	Time Out	Reason	Initials

PHOTOGRAPHY LOG			
Case number	Agency	Date	Time
Investigator		Equipment	
Crime type	Location		

Image number	Description of photo

PHOTOGRAPHY LOG

Case number	Agency	Date	Time
Investigator		Equipment	
Crime type	Location		

Image number	Description of photo

<table>
<tr><th colspan="6">PROPERTY RECORD AND RECEIPT</th></tr>
<tr><td colspan="3">Name of investigating officer</td><td colspan="2">PE</td><td>Case/Incident number</td></tr>
<tr><td colspan="3">Name of submitting officer</td><td colspan="2">PE</td><td>Lab number</td></tr>
<tr><td>Date</td><td colspan="2">Time</td><td colspan="3">From whom</td></tr>
<tr><td colspan="5">Location</td><td>County</td></tr>
<tr><td colspan="6">Witness of recovery</td></tr>
<tr><td colspan="5">Details</td><td>Offense</td></tr>
</table>

RMS	Item #	Description (include quantity, color, serial numbers and/or identifying marks)

REQUEST FOR LABORATORY EXAMINATION

PNW Forensics

Lab case # ______

Investigating officer	Email address
Contributing agency	County
Address	Telephone
Type of investigation	Agency case #
Victim name(s)	
Suspect name(s)	
Case/Incident summary	

Court date	Date of seizure	Assigned to

Item #	Description of the item submitted	Examination request

FORENSIC
CLASS
MOCK
CRIME
SCENE

IN PROGRESS

Lab 11-2 Indoors

OBJECTIVE Work together as a team and complete a major scene. This lab encompasses many of the disciplines that have been covered in class and the techniques that have been learned.

DIRECTIONS Divide the class into groups of 10 to 12. There are many different jobs to accomplish.

Mock Crime Scene

Case # PNW-050118

You have been called to the scene of a death investigation. The body of a 32-year-old male was found on the main floor (kitchen area) of his duplex. The officer in charge is Lieutenant Michael Brown from the Indiana State Police Criminal Investigation division.

The victim was found lying supine on the floor, his hands bound with duct tape at the wrists. There is a large pool of blood beneath his head. There did not appear to be any forced entry into the home. The house does not appear to be ransacked and there is no evidence of other major disturbances.

No one was home next door, but other detectives are canvassing the area for any witnesses.

Mock Crime Scene

Team: ___________
Team leader: ______________________________
Crime scene log: ____________________________
Photography unit: ____
Sketch team: ____
Evidence team: ____
Lifting and pouring: ____
Additional paperwork: ____

Your team must complete the following:

- Establish who will do each job.
- Establish a crime scene log for who enters and exits the scene.
- Photograph the scene (360 degrees): overall photos, all evidence, close-ups with scale. Complete photo log.
- Sketch the crime scene. This team will be responsible for measurements of the scene as well.
- "Collect" the evidence from the scene (don't actually take it out of the scene as other groups are still working). Seal packaging in proper evidence type (envelope, paper bag, plastic, can, etc.).
- Fingerprint the "marked area" (associated to your group number). Lift *all* latents in that area with tape lifters and place on backers and fill out info.
- Pour a cast of suspect shoe impression.

CRIME SCENE LOG

All personnel *must* sign before entering the crime scene.

Scene location: ______________________ Agency: ____________________

Date: _______________ Agency case number: ____________

Name/Rank	Agency	Initials	Time In	Time Out	Reason	Initials

PHOTOGRAPHY LOG

Case number	Agency	Date	Time
Investigator		Equipment	
Crime type	Location		

Image number	**Description of photo**

PROPERTY RECORD AND RECEIPT

Name of investigating officer	PE	Case/Incident number
Name of submitting officer	PE	Lab number

Date	Time	From whom

Location	County

Witness of recovery

Details	Offense

RMS	Item #	Description (include quantity, color, serial numbers and/or identifying marks)

REQUEST FOR LABORATORY EXAMINATION

PNW Forensics Lab case # ________

Investigating officer		Email address	
Contributing agency			County
Address			Telephone
Type of investigation			Agency case #
Victim name(s)			
Suspect name(s)			
Case/Incident summary			
Court date	Date of seizure		Assigned to

Item #	**Description of the item submitted**	**Examination request**

Index